AUGUSTA READ TH

SILENT MOON

FOR VIOLIN AND VIOLONCELLO

(SCORE AND PARTS)

ED 4522
First Printing: June 2013

ISBN: 978-1-4803-4142-5

G. SCHIRMER, Inc.

DISTRIBUTED BY

HAL•LEONARD®
CORPORATION
7777 W. BLUEMOUND RD. P.O. BOX 13819 MILWAUKEE, WI 53213

Composer's Note

The original version of Silent Moon for Violin and Viola (2006) was commissioned by
and dedicated with admiration and gratitude to Almita and Roland Vamos

The work is in three movements followed by a coda, played without pause.

I. Still: Soulful and Resonant
II. Energetic: Majestic and Dramatic
III. Suspended: Lyrical and Chant-like

"When twofold silence was the song of love"
*from the sonnet, *Silent Moon*
Dante Gabriel Rossetti (1828-1882)

Duration 7 minutes

The version for Violin and Viola is available: HL 50498779

Research has found the title of the sonnet to be "Silent Noon" however many versions use the title "Silent Moon." The sonnet which is attributed to Christina Georgina Rossetti in many editions, is the work of her brother, Dante Gabriel Rossetti.

Information on Augusta Read Thomas and her works is available at www.musicsalesclassical.com

with admiration and gratitude to Almita and Roland Vamos

SILENT MOON
(for Violin and Violonello)

Augusta Read Thomas
2006

I. Still: soulful and resonant

*: Perform standing when feasible.

**: Bowings, which are only suggestions, do not have to be used and grace notes should have a solid duration, never rushed nor slid through.

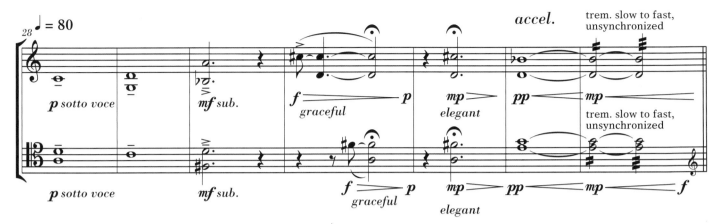

II. Energetic: majestic and dramatic ♩ = 88★

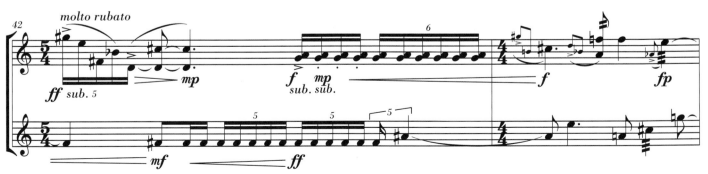

★ Grace notes come before the beat. Multiple grace notes are intended to slightly throw off the pulse, such that what comes after them
will be slightly late. Please vary the tremolo speeds so they each have an inner momentum. In measures 45-65 the fermatas should be semi-lunga
such that they suspend the energy in mid-air, and with surprise. Please vary the duration of the fermatas so that each one is unique.

AUGUSTA READ THOMAS

SILENT MOON
FOR VIOLIN AND VIOLONCELLO

VIOLONCELLO
(PLAYING SCORE)

ED 4522
First Printing: June 2013

ISBN: 978-1-4803-4142-5

G. SCHIRMER, Inc.

DISTRIBUTED BY

HAL•LEONARD®
CORPORATION
7777 W. BLUEMOUND RD. P.O. BOX 13819 MILWAUKEE, WI 53213

Violoncello

with admiration and gratitude to Almita and Roland Vamos

SILENT MOON
(for Violin and Violoncello)

I. Still: soulful and resonant
♩ = 63–69

Augusta Read Thomas
2006

*like bells, with a slight lift
between each new bell stroke*

*: Perform standing when feasible.

**: Bowings, which are only suggestions, do not have to be used and grace notes should have a solid duration, never rushed nor slid through.

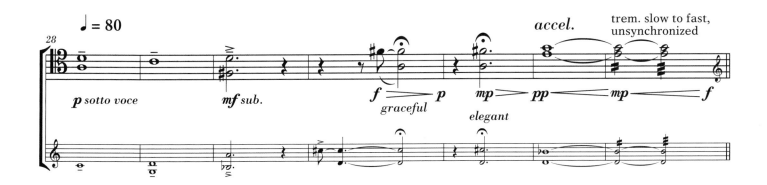

II. Energetic: majestic and dramatic ♩ = 88★

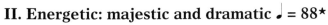

★ Grace notes come before the beat. Multiple grace notes are intended to slightly throw off the pulse, such that what comes after them will be slightly late. Please vary the tremolo speeds so they each have an inner momentum. In measures 45-65 the fermatas should be semi-lunga such that they suspend the energy in mid-air, and with surprise. Please vary the duration of the fermatas so that each one is unique.

Passionate; flexible ♩ = 50

allow time for the violin
to be rubato

rit.

cadenza-like; molto rubato

III. Suspended: lyrical and chant-like ♩ = 66–69

sul G & D

molto rubato
(D only is harmonic)

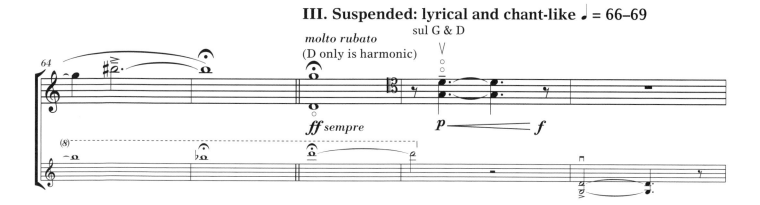

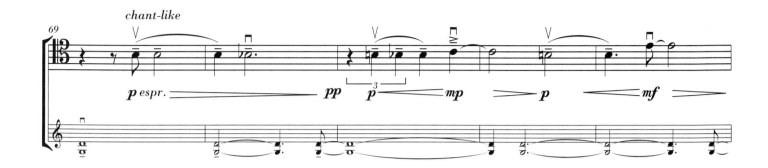

like bells, with a slight lift between each new bell stroke
sul G & D

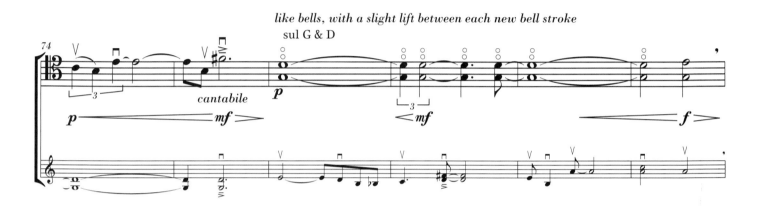

Coda: soul of the composition ♩ = 56

chant-like;sotto voce;
very little to non vibrato

…lean into the dissonances and make them special…

duration: 7 minutes

AUGUSTA READ THOMAS

SILENT MOON
FOR VIOLIN AND VIOLONCELLO

VIOLIN
(PLAYING SCORE)

ED 4522
First Printing: June 2013

ISBN: 978-1-4803-4142-5

G. SCHIRMER, Inc.

DISTRIBUTED BY

7777 W. BLUEMOUND RD. P.O. BOX 13819 MILWAUKEE, WI 53213

Violin

SILENT MOON
(for Violin and Violoncello)

Augusta Read Thomas
2006

I. Still: soulful and resonant

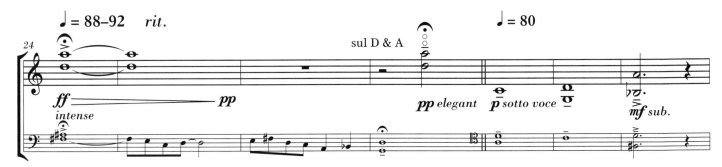

*: Perform standing when feasible.

**: Bowings, which are only suggestions, do not have to be used and grace notes should have a solid duration, never rushed nor slid through.

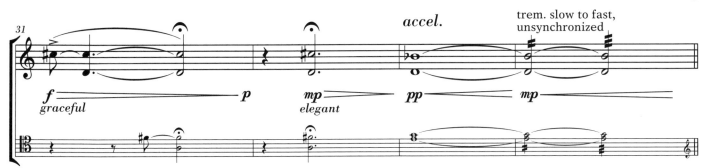

II. Energetic: majestic and dramatic ♩ = 88★

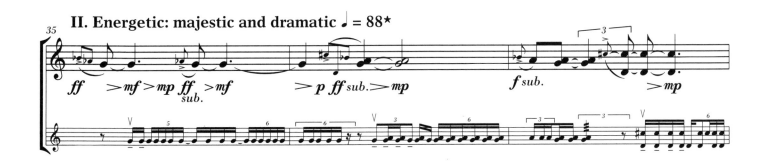

★ Grace notes come before the beat. Multiple grace notes are intended to slightly throw off the pulse, such that what comes after them will be slightly late. Please vary the tremolo speeds so they each have an inner momentum. In measures 45-65 the fermatas should be semi-lunga such that they suspend the energy in mid-air, and with surprise. Please vary the duration of the fermatas so that each one is unique.

III. Suspended: lyrical and chant-like ♩ = 66–69

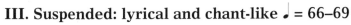

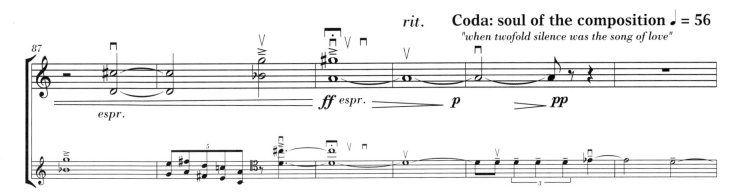

Vc.

...lean into the dissonances and make them special...

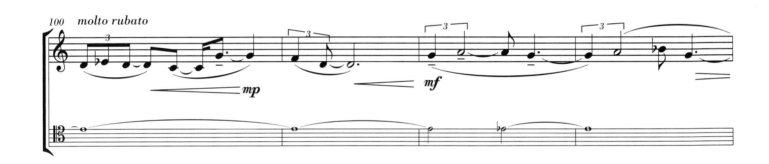

duration: 7 minutes

Molto Rubato ♩ = 60

Lyrical ♩ = 88

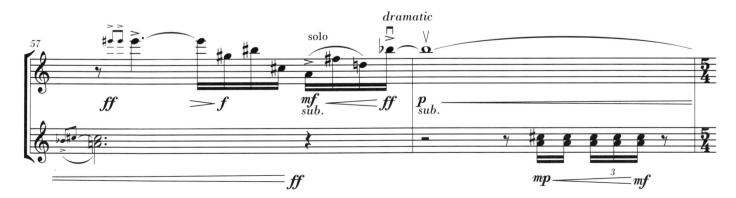

III. Suspended: lyrical and chant-like ♩ = 66–69

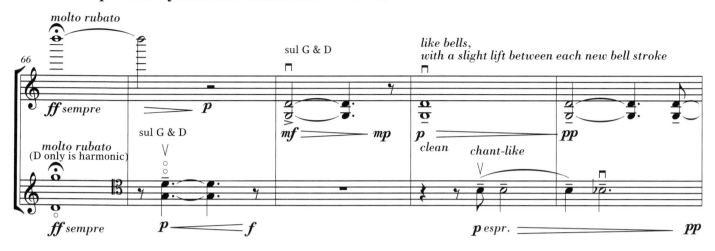

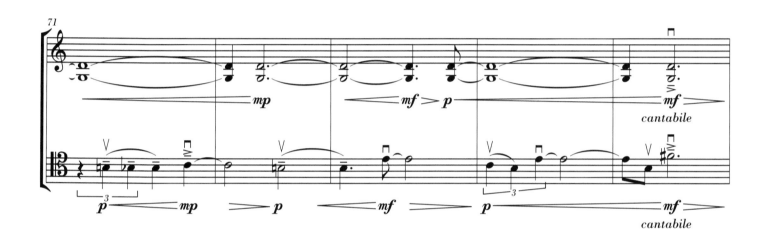

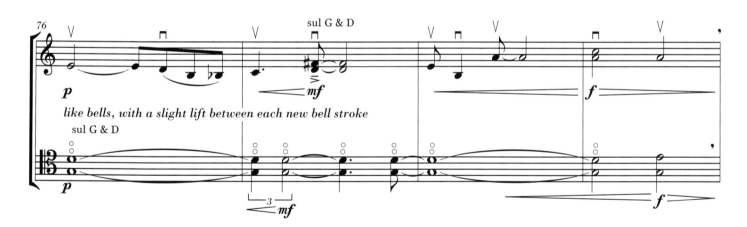

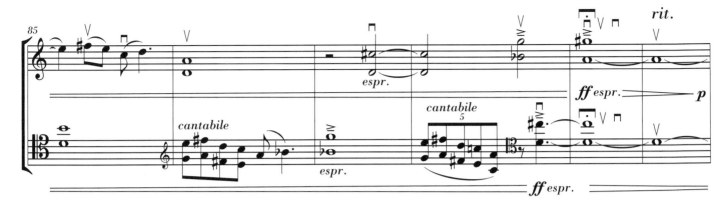

Coda: soul of the composition ♩ = 56

"when twofold silence was the song of love"

...lean into the dissonances and make them special...

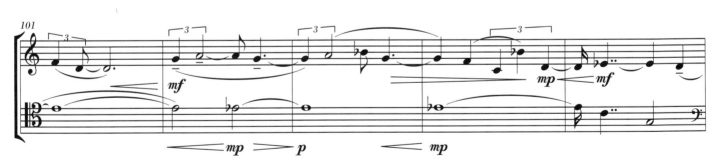

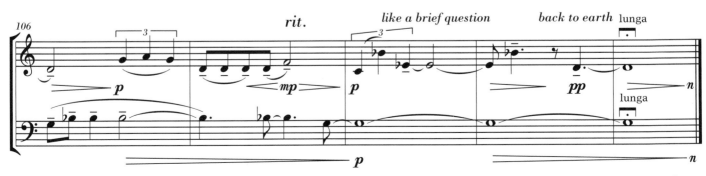

duration: 7 minutes